Paula on the Pony Farm
and Other English Stories

DIE AUTORINNEN

Kirsten Boie, eine der renommiertesten deutschen Autorinnen des modernen Kinder- und Jugendromans, wurde 1950 in Hamburg geboren, wo sie noch heute mit ihrer Familie lebt. Inzwischen sind von ihr weit mehr als sechzig Bücher erschienen und in zahlreiche Sprachen übersetzt worden.

Christine Nöstlinger, 1936 in Wien geboren, ist eine der profiliertesten Kinder- und Jugendbuchautorinnen des deutschen Sprachraums. Ihr Werk umfasst Bilderbücher, Erzählungen und Romane für Kinder und Jugendliche und Kinderlyrik. Sie wurde mit zahlreichen Preisen ausgezeichnet.

Ursel Scheffler wurde in Nürnberg geboren und studierte in München. Ihr erstes Kinderbuch schrieb sie 1975. Inzwischen hat die erfolgreiche Kinderbuchautorin fast 200 Bücher veröffentlicht, die man in 20 verschiedenen Sprachen lesen kann. Heute lebt sie mit ihrer Familie in Hamburg.

Ursel Scheffler • Christine Nöstlinger •
Kirsten Boie

Paula on the Pony Farm

and Other English Stories

Mit Illustrationen von Dagmar Henze,
Sabine Kraushaar und Silke Brix

cbj

cbj
ist der Kinder- und Jugendbuchverlag
in der Verlagsgruppe Random House

© **Mix**
Produktgruppe aus vorbildlich
bewirtschafteten Wäldern, kontrollierten
Herkünften und Recyclingholz oder -fasern
FSC www.fsc.org Zert.-Nr. SGS-COC-004278
© 1996 Forest Stewardship Council

Verlagsgruppe Random House FSC-DEU-0100
Das für dieses Buch verwendete FSC-zertifizierte
Papier *Profibulk* von Sappi liefert IGEPA

1. Auflage
Erstmals als cbj Taschenbuch Juni 2009
Gesetzt nach den Regeln der Rechtschreibreform
Ursel Scheffler, *Paula on the Pony Farm* © 2003 und 2004
Verlag Friedrich Oetinger GmbH, Hamburg
Die deutsche Originalausgabe erschien 2003 im Verlag
Friedrich Oetinger GmbH unter dem Titel »Paula auf dem Ponyhof«.
Christine Nöstlinger, *The Great Collector* © 2000 und 2003
Verlag Friedrich Oetinger GmbH, Hamburg
Die deutsche Originalausgabe erschien 2000 im Verlag
Friedrich Oetinger GmbH unter dem Titel »Rudi sammelt«.
Kirsten Boie, *Linnea Finds an Orphan Dog* © 2000 und 2002
Verlag Friedrich Oetinger GmbH, Hamburg
Die deutsche Originalausgabe erschien 2000 im Verlag
Friedrich Oetinger GmbH unter dem Titel
»Linnea findet einen Waisenhund«.
Alle Rechte dieser Ausgabe vorbehalten durch
cbj Verlag, München
Umschlagillustration: Dagmar Henze
Umschlaggestaltung: Basic-Book-Design, Karl Müller-Bussdorf
Innenillustrationen: Dagmar Henze, Sabine Kraushaar, Silke Brix
Übersetzung: David Henry Wilson
MI · Herstellung: CZ
Satz: Buch-Werkstatt GmbH, Bad Aibling
Druck und Bindung: Těšínska tiskárna, a.s., Český Těšín
ISBN: 978-3-570-22048-1
Printed in the Czech Republic

www.cbj-verlag.de

Inhalt

Ursel Scheffer
Paula on the Pony Farm   7

Christine Nöstlinger
The Great Collector   39

Kirsten Boie
Linnea Finds an Orphan Dog   71

Vokabelliste   103

Ursel Scheffler

Paula
on the Pony Farm

Pictures by
Dagmar Henze

Translated by
David Henry Wilson

"Pony farm! Pony farm!
I can go to the pony farm!"
cries Paula,
and goes dancing
around the flat.
"And that's where you belong,"
grumbles Titus.
"You're the silliest donkey I know."

"Grrr! You're just jealous!"
hisses Paula.
"Horses are only for girls,"
sneers Titus.
"And for cowboys and real men!"
cries Paula.
"You idiot!"

Then she rushes away.
Titus throws a trainer,
but it only hits the door.

What's really great
is that Paula's best friend Sarah
is allowed to come as well.
For hours the two girls
are on the phone,
talking about all the things
they have to pack.
"Jeans and a pullover will be
enough,"
says Paula in the end.
"Aunt Elfie has riding helmets
and boots."

Paula's favourite aunt
has just set up
a pony farm for children.
Paula and Sarah
are the first visitors.
Aunt Elfie is standing
at the farm gate
when Paula's dad
brings the two girls.

"Are the ponies in the stable?"
asks Paula.
"They're still in the field
behind the house," says Aunt Elfie.

"This one's my favourite,"
says Paula.
She's standing in front of
a brown pony
with a white blaze.
"His name is Shooting Star!"
"And what's the name
of the white pony?"
asks Sarah.
"Snoopy," says Paula.
She waves a carrot in the air.
Snoopy comes running.

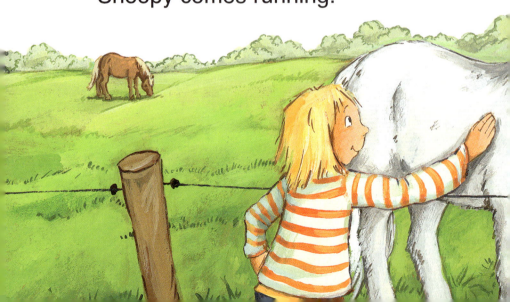

He pushes his muzzle
into Paula's hand.
It's warm and soft.
"Can we go riding straight away?"
asks Paula.
"That's all right with me,"
says Aunt Elfie.
"Jack will help you saddle up.
Boots and helmets
are in the changing room."

Paula likes Jack.
He's her cousin.
"Jack's five years older
and five times nicer than Titus,"
Paula tells Sarah.

Jack taught Paula
to ride some time ago.
Now he helps Sarah
climb into the saddle.

"Snoopy is nice.
But hold tight all the same,"
Jack tells Sarah.
Then he rides away
with the two girls.

Sarah went to a pony farm
last year too.
But she still can't ride
as well as Paula.
And so Jack
stays very close to her
all the time.

They trot for a while
alongside the stream.
A rabbit hops across the track.

Snoopy is startled
and suddenly stops.
Sarah falls headfirst into the grass.
Luckily she's all right.
"It's a good thing
you've got your helmet on!"
says Jack, relieved,
and helps her to stand up.

Paula is a little bit jealous
because Jack is only paying attention
to Sarah.
But then he rides
to Paula's favourite spot,
a little glade in the forest.

A few obstacles
have been built there,
made out of tree trunks.
Paula is allowed to jump over them
on Shooting Star.
Sarah isn't allowed yet.
"Maybe in two or three days,"
says Jack, the riding instructor.

When the sun sets
behind the edge of the forest,
they ride back to the farm.

"It was wonderful!"
says Sarah to Jack,
and her eyes are shining.
"Yes, it was wonderful,"
says Paula,
and puts both her arms
round Shooting Star's neck.

"The fun comes first," says Jack,
"and then comes the work."
Now they have
to take off the saddles,
rub down the ponies,
give them food and water,
and scrape the hooves.
Paula spreads some fresh straw
round the stalls.

Then they lead the ponies
into the stable.
Jack locks the stable door.
"But you don't normally do that,
do you?" asks Paula in surprise.
"It's better," says Jack seriously.
"For some time now
there's been a horse thief
going around the area.
Yesterday
a pregnant mare
was stolen
from our neighbours."

"What does pregnant actually mean?"
asks Sarah in the evening,
when they're brushing their teeth.
"Pregnant means
the mare is expecting a baby,"
explains Paula.

The girls lie awake
for a long time
and tell each other stories.
Finally they go to sleep.

Then in the middle
of the night,
Paula hears
strange noises.

She climbs out of bed
and runs to the window.
Oh dear!
A dark figure is creeping
across the yard.
The light from a torch
shines on the stable door.

"Sarah, wake up!"
cries Paula nervously,
and pulls the cover
off Sarah's bed.
"There's someone in the yard!
I'm sure it's the horse thief!
We must wake Aunt Elfie up!"

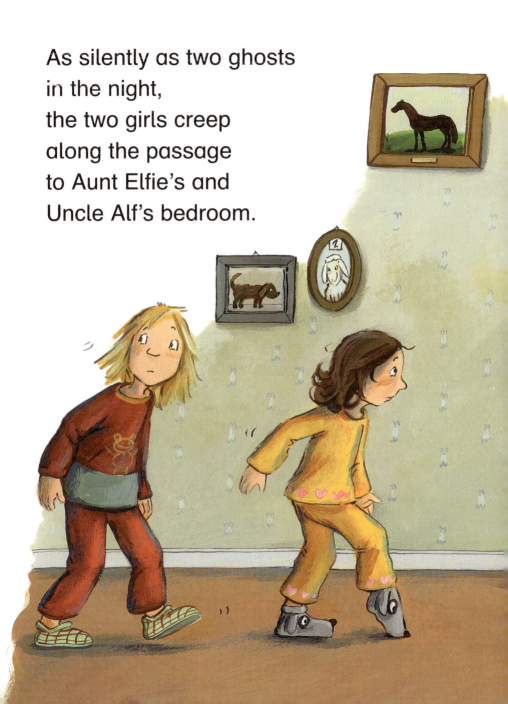

Carefully they open the door.
"Aunt Elfie? Uncle Alf?"
whispers Paula.
Nobody answers.
Paula puts on the light.
Aunt Elfie's and Uncle Alf's beds
are empty!
Could the thief
have kidnapped them both?
"What shall we do now?"
asks Sarah, frightened.
"Call the police!"
says Paula, resolutely.
"Come with me!
The telephone's in the kitchen!"
On tiptoe the two of them
creep downstairs.

There's a light on in the kitchen,
and there's a smell of fresh coffee.
Aunt Elfie is standing by the oven.
"What are you doing here?"
she cries in surprise
when the two girls
suddenly appear in the kitchen.

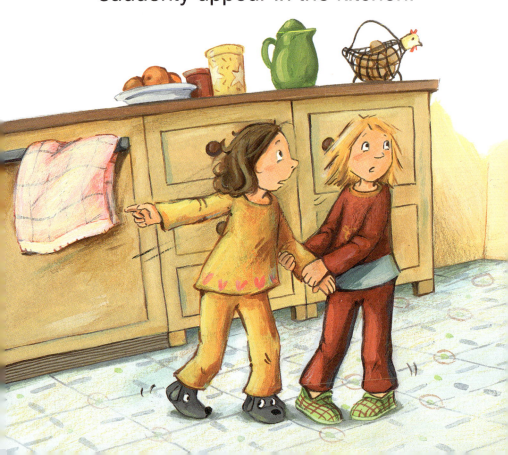

"A thief!" whispers Paula.
"Over there at the stable."
But Aunt Elfie just laughs
and says:
"Come with me.
I know the thief."
They go across the yard.

The stable door is just slightly ajar.
Standing in the stall
next to Snoopy
are Uncle Alf and Jack.
And the stranger
is kneeling there too!
He is helping a little foal
onto its feet.
"The thief is our vet,"
explains Aunt Elfie.
"Senta has had her foal
before we expected it."

"We need to give
the little one a name,"
says Uncle Alf.
"What about Robber?"
says Jack, and grins.

"We need a name
beginning with A!
Because the name of the foal's father
is Amadeus,
and so the foal's name
must also begin with an A,"
says Uncle Alf.
"Ali Baba!" cries Paula.
Everyone agrees.

The little robber Ali
is still standing
on very wobbly legs.
His mother lovingly licks him clean.
"Right, the two of them
need some peace and quiet now,"
says the vet firmly.
"And I think you do too."

"I'm not tired at all!"
says Sarah.
"I'd really like to sleep
with Ali in the stable!"
"But I'm going to bed,"
cries Paula happily.
"Because I think
straw is very prickly
on the bottom!"

Christine Nöstlinger

The Great Collector

Pictures by
Sabine Kraushaar

Translated by
David Henry Wilson

This is Rudi,

and Dad

and Mum,

and Granny.

Rudi's dad collected stamps.
As Rudi thought
that everything his dad did
was great,
he also wanted to collect something.
But stamps were too small for him,
and also a bit boring.

Rudi thought about it every day:
What could I collect?
He didn't want
to ask his dad.
Dad would certainly
have advised him to collect stamps.
But one Sunday
he suddenly knew.
This is how it came about:
Rudi was thirsty,
and took the bottle of apple juice
out of the fridge.

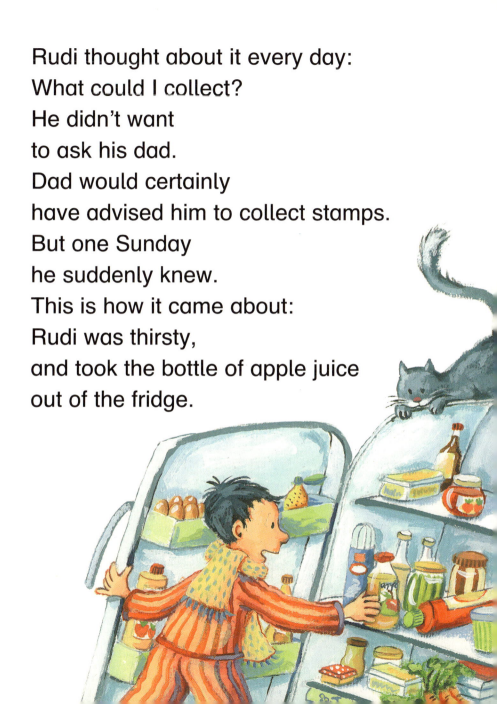

As he had a cold,
Mum called out,
"The juice is much too cold!"
She ran some warm water
into the sink
and put the bottle in it.
"It'll only take a minute,"
she said,
"and then the juice
will be OK for you."

After a minute,
not only was the juice OK,
but the label
had also peeled off the bottle.
Then Rudi decided:
I'll be a label collector!

Dad was extremely happy
that Rudi
was now a collector, too.
He gave Rudi a pile of
clear folders and said:
"Put the labels in the folders,
so that they'll always stay
beautiful."

Mum just murmured,
"So now I've got
another idiot in the family!"
But that didn't worry Rudi.
If Mum thought
Dad was an idiot,
Rudi was happy
to be an idiot.
Rudi started collecting
straight away.

In the rubbish bin
he found four beer bottles,
and in the dining room
a bottle of schnapps.
Actually this wasn't quite empty,
but Dad called out,
"Collectors must help one another,"
and drank up the rest of the
schnapps.

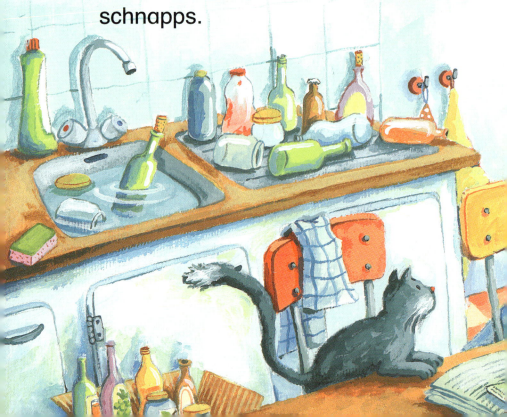

Rudi carried the bottles
into the kitchen.
He filled the sink with water,
and let them float
until the labels slipped off.
He laid the wet labels
on the kitchen table to dry.

When they were dry,
he put them
in the clear folders.
Dad praised him:
"Great work
for the first day!"

At supper Rudi asked,
"From now on could you drink
a different beer every day?
Because of the labels."
"Of course!" said Dad.
"We'll drink our way
through every sort of beer."

But as Rudi didn't want
just beer labels,
he got into terrible trouble
with Mum on Monday.

In order to get hold of new labels,
he emptied the whole fridge.
He thought that whatever
was in the bottles
would be obvious,
even if there were
no labels on them.
The result was a super collection.

Afterwards the kitchen table
was overflowing
with soaking wet labels
from wine bottles,
lemonade bottles,
ketchup bottles, liqueur bottles,
vinegar bottles and oil bottles.

When Mum saw the kitchen table,
she went hopping mad.
Now she wouldn't know
what bottle contained the vinegar
and what bottle contained the wine.
Instead of ketchup
Rudi would get chilli sauce
on his chips.
Then he'd soon see
what a mess he'd made!

Dad took Rudi's side.
"You've got no feelings
for us collectors,"
he said.
"We can't worry
about such trivialities!"
And he advised Rudi,
"Go round the other apartments
and ask people
to give you their empty bottles."

Rudi did that on Tuesday,
and by Wednesday
there were eight big carrier bags
standing outside the door.
They contained nothing
but beer bottles.
Unfortunately, only those with labels
that Rudi already had.
And of course a collector
only needs one label of each kind.

"What a load of rubbish!"
complained Rudi.
"Exactly!" said Mum.
"And now take the rubbish
to where it belongs!"
Instead of watching TV,
Rudi had to take those stupid bottles
to the bottle bank.
Three times he had to go there,
until he'd got rid of them all.

On Friday the neighbour
brought a large bag
of old, dusty bottles.
"I cleared out the cellar for you,"
he said.

The bottles were so dirty
that Rudi couldn't see
whether they had nice labels or not.

He dragged the bag
into the bathroom
and washed fifty bottles clean.
Only one had a pretty label.
Rudi peeled it off,
and then he cleaned the bathroom
because the dirty bottles
had made a mess
on the floor tiles.

Then Rudi carried fifty bottles
to the bottle bank.
Afterwards he was worn out.
And that was what happened
every day.
Someone always put empty bottles
outside the door.

It really got on Mum's nerves.
"It's as if we were a rubbish tip!"
she yelled.
"And whenever
I want to take a bath,
there are bottles in the tub."
Dad said proudly,
"My son takes
after his father!"
And then he gave Rudi
another pile of clear folders.

But Rudi was in despair.
He hadn't imagined
that collecting would be like this.
It was nothing but total stress!
He spent all his spare time on it.
And out of a hundred bottles,
there were only three
with labels that were any good.

Besides that,
Rudi thought to himself:
People are bringing me
their bottles because it's easier
than taking them to the bottle bank.

He felt really sick every morning
when he saw the new delivery.
But he didn't want to admit it.
He thought:
Then Dad will be
disappointed in me
and he'll think
that I don't take after him.

And so Rudi went on collecting,
and was really miserable doing it.
But then came Mum's birthday.
Rudi asked Granny,
"What should I give Mum?
I can't think of anything,
and I haven't got any money either."

Granny said, "I know something
that wouldn't cost any money.
But you certainly
won't be able to do it."
"Tell me!" cried Rudi.
"No, no," said Granny,
"it would be too much
of a sacrifice!"
"Tell me!" cried Rudi again.

Then at last Granny said,
"Your label-collecting
is driving your Mum crazy.
If it goes on like this,
she says,
she'll have a breakdown."
Rudi thought about it.
Long and hard.

Then he asked,
"Do you mean
I should stop collecting labels?
That's the present
I should give her?"

Granny sighed and said,
"I don't suppose a child
who takes after his father
could manage that."
"Yes, I can," cried Rudi,
"I'll manage that for Mum!"

Then he took a sheet of paper
and wrote on it:

He stuck the sheet of paper
on the front door.
Dad read the notice
when he came home
from work.

"Rudi, Rudi!" he cried.
"What's the matter?"
"That's my birthday present
for Mum," said Rudi.
"To stop her having a breakdown."
Dad gazed at him and,
deeply moved, said,
"I'm proud of you.
You're a better man
than I am!
To give up collecting
just out of love,
I'd never be able to manage that!"

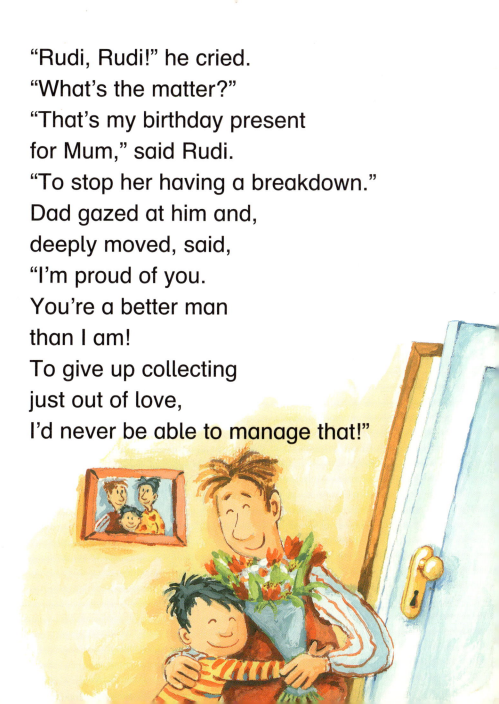

Rudi went a little red
in the face.
But then he thought:
Mum will be saved
from her breakdown,
I'll be free of those stupid bottles,
and Dad won't be
disappointed in me.
So everything's perfect.

Kirsten Boie

Linnea Finds an Orphan Dog

Pictures by
Silke Brix

Translated by
David Henry Wilson

Some children are lucky.
They have a horse,
or a dog,
or some other nice animal.
But Linnea has nothing at all.

All she has is Magnus,
who is seven,
and Anna,
who is nearly eleven.
But of course
brothers and sisters
are not as good
as real animals.

At least Linnea can sometimes
play with Magnus.
He's not as good
as a dog,
but all the same he's better
than little Erdem
from the fourth floor.
He starts howling
even if you only touch him.

"And chocolate?"
asks Linnea.
"Is that there too, Magnus?
Or jelly babies, perhaps?"
"That's not there,"
says Magnus,
and shakes his head.
"I can read that.
And now I'm going in.
If you want to come with me,
you can."

But Linnea
certainly doesn't want to.
Boring margarine
and greaseproof paper –
Magnus should buy those
on his own.
Linnea prefers
to have fun outside.
And she knows exactly
what she's going to do.

Next to the shop entrance
there's a hook.
People always tie
their dogs to it.
There's a dog
waiting there now –
a huge, fat one
which keeps sticking
its tongue out,
and looks so sad
and so lonely.

"Well, doggy?" says Linnea, and sits down on the path beside him.
"Are you all alone? Haven't you got anyone in the world?"

The dog wags
his tail so wildly
that Linnea knows:
The dog at the door
is really all alone,
and has been waiting just for her,
and would like to be *her* dog.
So she unhooks him.
Now the dog
is no longer alone and lonely,
and he joyfully
licks Linnea's face all over.

Linnea thinks
that now
she's a good person,
if she makes
such a sad dog happy.
But then Magnus
comes out of the shop and says
that Linnea
can't just simply steal
a strange dog.

"He belongs to someone!"
says Magnus.
"You can see for yourself!"
But Linnea shakes her head.
"He's an orphan dog!"
she cries.
"And *you* can see that
for *yourself*, stupid!"

And then she runs home,
and the orphan dog
really runs
quite happily after her,
and wags his tail.

"You see!"
says Linnea,
when she gets
to the front door.
"Look how happy he is."

Then Magnus pulls
a very thoughtful face,
and he says:
"Well, maybe there are sometimes
lonely dogs,
and they haven't got a father
or a mother,
a mistress
or a master."

"Poor little dog!"
says Magnus,
and looks at the licence disc.
"Now you've got us."

"He hasn't got *you*!"
says Linnea.
"He's my dog!
After all,
I found him!"

But then she thinks
that it might be more fun
if Magnus also plays with them.
"If you're nice,
you can hold him,"
says Linnea.
"And you can think
that he's your dog.
But you mustn't *say* so."
And she gives the leash to Magnus.

Just as Magnus is about
to take the dog for a little walk
and to think
that the dog is his,
Anna suddenly
comes out of the house.

"What sort of dog
is that?"
asks Anna.
"Where did you get him from?"

Magnus makes an angry face,
and Linnea says
that it's an orphan dog.
Anna can surely see that
for herself.
"An orphan dog!"
cries Linnea.
"And you don't want us
to let him starve, do you?"

"Don't talk rubbish,"
says Anna.
"There are no orphan dogs,
stupid!
And anyway,
this one's got a dog licence!
You stole him!"
At this moment the dog
is licking
Linnea's face again,
and is also wagging
his tail again very sweetly.

"Look!"
cries Linnea.
"How he loves me!"
But of course as usual
Magnus has to take Anna's side.

"No, come on, Linnea,"
he says.
"If the dog belongs to somebody,
then that person
must be very sad now.
If we've stolen
their dog."
Then Linnea looks
at him really angrily and says
that the dog *is* an orphan.
Magnus will soon see for himself.

But she does go back
to the shop
with Magnus and the dog
– though very slowly.
And there really
is an old lady standing there,
and she looks very upset.

When the dog
sees the old lady,
suddenly he's not an orphan
any more.
He pulls himself free,
and runs and runs,
and then leaps up high,
and almost knocks
the old lady over.

"Oh Bonzo,
you naughty boy!"
says the old lady,
and keeps stroking
the dog's head.
"Did you pull
your leash loose again?
You mustn't do that!"

But then she suddenly sees
Linnea and Magnus.
They are standing there watching.
"He cheated us!"
says Linnea angrily.
"He's not an orphan dog at all!"
And she may even have
to have a little cry now.

"So you two
caught my Bonzo,"
says the old lady.
"Well, that was kind of you!
Now perhaps
you can help me again.
Both my hands are full,
so maybe you could take
Bonzo for me."
"May we also think
that he's our dog?"
asks Linnea.

"People can think
what they want to,"
says the old lady.
"Thoughts are free."
And so Linnea and Magnus
take the leash together,
and think to themselves
that Bonzo is their dog,
and their dog alone.

And perhaps Bonzo
is even thinking that, too,
because he runs and jumps around
and looks very happy
all the time.

"You know what, Magnus?"
says Linnea,
when they go home later.
"He wasn't an orphan dog
after all.
And so we can't be
his Mummy
and his Daddy.
But we can be his Auntie
and Uncle."

Magnus nods.
He would like
to be a dog's uncle.
"Tomorrow,"
says Magnus contently.
They'll certainly go
and see him again.

Vokabelliste

a

a [eɪ], [ə]	ein(e)
a bit [ə] [bɪt]	ein bisschen, etwas
a few [ə] [fjuː]	ein paar
a hundred [ə] [ˈhʌndrɪd]	(ein)hundert
a load [ə] [ləʊd]	~~eine~~ Menge
able to do [ˈeɪbl] [tuː] [duː]	etwas schaffen, können (to be able to do)
about [əˈbaʊt]	(dar)über
across [əˈkrɒs]	(quer) über
actually [ˈæktjʊəlɪ]	tatsächlich, eigentlich
admit [ədˈmɪt]	zugeben (to admit)
advised [ədˈvaɪzd]	geraten (to advise = raten)
after [ˈɑːftəʳ]	danach, nach
after all [ˈɑːftəʳ][ɔːl]	schließlich
afterwards [ˈɑːftəwədz]	nachher, danach
again [əˈgen]	wieder, erneut
agrees [əˈgriːz]	er, sie, es ist einverstanden (to agree = einverstanden sein)
air [ɛəʳ]	die Luft
ajar [əˈdʒɑːʳ]	angelehnt, einen Spalt offen
all [ɔːl]	alle, alles, ganz
all over [ɔːl][ˈəʊvəʳ]	überall
all right [ɔːl] [raɪt]	okay, in Ordnung
all the same [ɔːl] [ðə] [seɪm]	trotzdem, alles in allem
all the time [ɔːl][ðə][taɪm]	immer
allowed [əˈlaʊd]	er, sie, es darf (to be allowed = dürfen)

almost [ˈɔːlməʊst]	beinahe, fast
alone [əˈləʊn]	allein, alleine
along [əˈlɒŋ]	über, entlang
alongside [əˈlɒŋˈsaɪd]	am, neben
already [ɔːlˈredɪ]	schon
also [ˈɔːlsəʊ]	auch
always [ˈɔːlweɪz]	ewig, immer, jederzeit
am [æm]	bin (to be = sein)
an [æn]	ein, eine
and [ænd]	und
angrily [ˈæŋgrɪlɪ]	böse
angry [ˈæŋgrɪ]	böse
animal [ˈænɪməl]	das Tier
another [əˈnʌðəʳ]	ein(e) andere(r, s), weitere(r, s)
answers [ˈɑːnsɪz]	er, sie, es antwortet (to answer = antworten)
any [ˈenɪ]	einige, etwas, irgendein(e)
any more [ˈenɪ] [mɔːʳ]	keine … mehr, nicht mehr
anyone [ˈenɪwʌn]	irgendjemand
anyway [ˈenɪweɪ]	jedenfalls
apartments [əˈpɑːtmənts]	die Wohnungen (apartment = die Wohnung)
appear [əˈpɪəʳ]	erscheinen, auftauchen (to appear)
apple juice [ˈæpl] [dʒuːs]	der Apfelsaft
are [ɑːʳ]	sind (to be = sein)
area [ˈɛərɪə]	die Gegend
arms [ɑːmz]	die Arme (arm = der Arm)
around [əˈraʊnd]	herum, rum

as [æz]	so, wie, weil
as good as [æz][gʊd][æz]	so gut wie
as if [æz] [ɪf]	als ob
as usual [æz]['juːʒəl]	wie gewöhnlich
as well [æz] [wel]	auch
as well as [æz] [wel] [æz]	so gut wie
asked [aːskt]	bat, fragte (to ask = bitten, fragen)
asks [aːsks]	er, sie, es bittet, fragt (to ask = bitten, fragen)
at [æt]	an, am, beim, bei
at all [æt][ɔːl]	überhaupt
at last [æt] [laːst]	endlich, schließlich
at least [æt] [liːst]	wenigstens
attention [ə'tenʃən]	die Aufmerksamkeit
aunt [aːnt]	die Tante
auntie ['aːntɪ]	das Tantchen (Koseform für: aunt = die Tante)
awake [ə'weɪk]	wach
away [ə'weɪ]	weg

b

baby ['beɪbɪ]	das Baby
back [bæk]	zurück
bag [bæg]	die Tasche, die Tüte
bathroom ['baːθruːm]	das Badezimmer
be [biː]	sein (to be)
be free of [biː] [friː] [ɒv]	los sein, frei sein von
beautiful ['bjuːtɪfʊl]	schön
because [bɪ'kɒz]	weil
because of [bɪ'kɒz] [ɒv]	wegen, aufgrund

become [bɪˈkʌm]	werden (to become)
bed [bed]	das Bett
bedroom [ˈbedruːm]	das Schlafzimmer
beds [bedz]	die Betten (bed = das Bett)
been [biːn]	gewesen (to be = sein)
beer bottles [bɪəˈ] [ˈbɒtls]	die Bierflaschen (beer bottle = die Bierflasche)
before [bɪˈfɔːˈ]	(be)vor
begin, beginning [bɪˈgɪn] [bɪˈgɪnɪŋ]	anfangen, beginnen (to begin)
behind [bɪˈhaɪnd]	hinter
belong [bɪˈlɒŋ]	hingehörst (to belong = (hin)gehören)
belongs [bɪˈlɒŋz]	er, sie, es gehört (to belong = gehören)
beside [bɪˈsaɪd]	neben
besides [bɪˈsaɪdz]	außerdem
best [best]	beste(r, s)
better [ˈbetəˈ]	besser (good = gut)
big [bɪg]	groß
birthday [ˈbɜːθdeɪ]	der Geburtstag
blaze [bleɪz]	die Blesse
boots [buːts]	die Stiefel (boot = der Stiefel)
boring [ˈbɔːrɪŋ]	langweilig
both [bəʊθ]	beide
bottle [ˈbɒtl]	die Flasche
bottle bank [ˈbɒtl] [bæŋk]	der Altglas-Container
bottom [ˈbɒtəm]	der Po

boy [bɔɪ]	der Junge
breakdown [ˈbreɪkdaʊn]	die Krise, der Zusammenbruch
bringing [ˈbrɪŋɪŋ]	bringen (to bring = bringen)
brings [brɪŋz]	er, sie, es bringt (to bring = bringen)
brothers [ˈbrʌθəʳz]	die Brüder (brother = der Bruder)
brought [brɔːt]	brachte (to bring = bringen)
brown [braʊn]	braun(e, er, es)
brushing [ˈbrʌʃɪŋ]	putzen (to brush)
built [bɪlt]	gebaut (to build = bauen)
but [bʌt]	aber, (je)doch
buy [baɪ]	kaufen (to buy)
buys [baɪz]	er, sie, es kauft (to buy = kaufen)
by [baɪ]	am, bis, durch, von

C

call [kɔːl]	rufen (to call)
called out [kɔːld] [aʊt]	rief (aus) (to call out = (aus)rufen)
came [keɪm]	kam (to come = kommen)
came home [keim] [həʊm]	kam heim (to come home = heimkommen)
can [kæn]	kann, können
can't [kaːnt]	können nicht (Kurzform von: cannot)
can't think of anything [kaːnt] [θɪnk] [ɒv] [ˈænɪθɪŋ]	fällt nichts ein
carefully [ˈkɛəfəlɪ]	vorsichtig

carried ['kærɪd]	schleppte, trug (to carry = schleppen, tragen)
carrier bags ['kærɪəʳ] [bægz]	die Tragetaschen (carrier bag = die Tragetasche)
carrot ['kærət]	die Möhre
caught [kɔːt]	fingen (to catch = fangen)
cellar ['seləʳ]	der Keller
certainly ['sɜːtənlɪ]	sicher, sicherlich
changing room ['tʃeɪndʒɪŋ] [ruːm]	die Reitkammer, der Umkleideraum
cheated ['tʃiːtɪd]	reingelegt (to cheat = reinlegen)
child [tʃaɪld]	das Kind
children ['tʃɪldrən]	die Kinder (child = das Kind)
chilli sauce ['tʃɪlɪ] [sɔːs]	die Chili-Soße
chips [tʃɪps]	die Pommes frites
chocolate ['tʃɒklɪt]	die Schokolade
clean [kliːn]	sauber
cleaned [kliːnd]	putzte, reinigte (to clean = putzen, reinigen)
clear folders [klɪəʳ] ['fəʊldəz]	die Klarsichthüllen (clear folder = die Klarsichthülle)
cleared out [klɪəʳd] [aʊt]	aufgeräumt, ausgeräumt (to clear out = aufräumen, ausräumen)
climb [klaɪm]	steigen, klettern (to climb)
climbs [klaɪmz]	er, sie, es steigt (to climb = steigen)
close to [kləʊs] [tuː]	nah, dicht bei
coffee ['kɒfɪ]	der Kaffee
cold [kəʊld]	die Erkältung; kalt

collect [kəˈlekt]	sammeln (to collect)
collected [kəˈlektɪd]	sammelte (to collect = sammeln)
collecting [kəˈlektɪŋ]	das Sammeln, zu sammeln (to collect = sammeln)
collection [kəˈlekʃən]	die Sammlung
collector [kəˈlektəʳ]	der Sammler
come [kʌm]	kommen, komm, kommt (to come = kommen)
come on! [kʌm][ɒn]	komm schon!
comes [kʌmz]	er, sie, es kommt (to come = kommen)
comes running [kʌmz] [ˈrʌnɪŋ]	kommt gelaufen (to come running = gelaufen kommen)
comes up with [kʌmz] [ʌp] [wɪð]	fällt ein, kommt auf (to come up with = einen Einfall haben, auf etwas kommen)
complained [kɒmˈpleɪnd]	schimpfte, beschwerte sich (to complain = schimpfen, sich beschweren)
contained [kɒnˈteɪnd]	enthielt (to contain = enthalten)
contently [kənˈtentlɪ]	zufrieden
cost [kɒst]	(Geld) kosten (to cost)
could [kʊd]	könnte, konnte (can = können)
couldn't [ˈkʊdnt]	konnte nicht (Kurzform von: could not)
cousin [ˈkʌzn]	der Cousin, der Vetter
cover [ˈkʌvəʳ]	die Bettdecke

cowboys ['kaʊbɔɪz]	die Cowboys (cowboy = der Cowboy)
creep [kriːp]	schleichen (to creep)
(is) creeping [ɪz] ['kriːpɪŋ]	er, sie, es schleicht (to be creeping = schleichen)
cried [kraɪd]	rief, schrie, weinte (to cry = rufen, schreien, weinen)
cries [kraɪz]	er, sie, es ruft, schreit, weint (to cry = rufen, schreien, weinen)
cry [kraɪ]	rufen, schreien, weinen (to cry)

d

dad [dæd]	der Vater, der Papa
daddy ['dædɪ]	der Papa
dancing ['daːnsɪŋ]	tanzen (to dance)
dark [daːk]	dunkel, dunkle(r, s)
day [deɪ]	der Tag
days [deɪz]	die Tage (day = der Tag)
decided [dɪ'saɪdɪd]	beschloss, entschied (to decide = beschließen, entscheiden)
deeply moved ['diːplɪ] [muːvd]	tief gerührt
delivery [dɪ'lɪvərɪ]	die Lieferung
did [dɪd]	tat (to do = tun)
didn't want ['dɪdənt] [wɒnt]	wollte nicht (Kurzform von: did not)
different ['dɪfrənt]	andere(r, s), unterschiedlich(e, r, s)
dining room ['daɪnɪŋ] [ruːm]	das Esszimmer
dirty ['dɜːtɪ]	dreckig, schmutzig

disappointed in [ˌdɪsəˈpɔɪntɪd] [ɪn]	enttäuscht von
do you mean [duː] [juː] [miːn]	meinst du (to mean = meinen)
do you? [duː] [juː]	oder?
do, doing [duː] [ˈduːɪŋ]	machst, macht, machen, tun (to do)
does [dʌz]	er, sie, es tut (to do = tun, machen)
doesn't want to [ˈdʌznt][wɒnt][tuː]	er, sie, es will nicht (Kurzform von: does not)
dog [dɒg]	der Hund
doggy [ˈdɒgɪ]	das Hündchen
don't [dəʊnt]	tust nicht, nicht tun (Kurzform von: do not)
donkey [ˈdɒnkɪ]	der Esel
door [dɔːˈ]	die Tür
down [daʊn]	unten
downstairs [ˌdaʊnˈstɛəz]	treppab
dragged [drægd]	schleppte (to drag = schleppen)
drank up [dræŋk] [ʌp]	trank aus (to drink up = austrinken)
drink [drɪŋk]	trinken (to drink)
drink our way through [drɪŋk] [aʊə] [weɪ] [θruː]	wir trinken uns durch …
driving … crazy [ˈdraɪvɪŋ] [ˈkreɪzɪ]	(jemanden) verrückt machen (to drive someone crazy = jemanden verrückt machen)
dry [draɪ]	trocknen (to dry); trocken
during [ˈdjʊərɪŋ]	während
dusty [ˈdʌstɪ]	verstaubt, staubig

each [iːtʃ]	jede, jeder, jedes
each other [iːtʃ] ['ʌðəʳ]	gegenseitig
easier ['iːzɪəʳ]	leichter(e, r, s) (easy = leicht)
edge [edʒ]	der Rand
eight [eɪt]	acht
either ['aɪθəʳ]	auch kein(e, r, s), auch nicht
eleven [ɪ'levn]	elf
emptied ['emptɪd]	räumte, leerte (aus) (to empty = (aus)räumen, (aus)leeren)
empty ['emptɪ]	leer
end [end]	das Ende
enough [ɪ'nʌf]	genug
entrance ['entrəːns]	der Eingang
even ['iːvən]	sogar
even if ['iːvən] [ɪf]	auch wenn
evening ['iːvnɪŋ]	der Abend
every ['evrɪ]	jede(r, s)
everyone ['evrɪwʌn]	jede(r)
everything ['evrɪθɪŋ]	alles
everything's ['evrɪθɪŋz]	alles ist (Kurzform von: everything is)
exactly! [ɪg'zæktlɪ]	exakt! genau!
expected [ɪk'spektɪd]	erwartet (to expect = erwarten)
explains [ɪk'spleɪnz]	er, sie, es erklärt (to explain = erklären)
extremely [ɪk'striːmlɪ]	riesig, äußerst, extrem
eyes [aɪz]	die Augen (eye = das Auge)

f

face [feɪs]	das Gesicht
falls [fɔːlz]	er, sie, es fällt (to fall = fallen)
family ['fæmɪlɪ]	die Familie
farm [faːm]	der Bauernhof
fat [fæt]	dick, fett
father ['faːðəʳ]	der Vater
favourite ['feɪvərɪt]	der, die, das Liebling(s-)
feelings ['fiːlɪŋz]	das Herz, die Gefühle feeling = das Gefühl)
feet [fiːt]	die Füße (foot = der Fuß)
felt [felt]	fühlte (to feel = fühlen)
field [fiːld]	die Weide
fifty ['fɪftɪ]	fünfzig
figure ['fɪgəʳ]	die Gestalt
filled [fɪld]	füllte (to fill = füllen)
finally ['faɪnəlɪ]	endlich, schließlich
finds [faɪndz]	er, sie, es findet (to find = finden)
firmly ['fɜːmlɪ]	bestimmt
first [fɜːst]	erste(r, s), zuerst
five [faɪv]	fünf
flat [flæt]	die Wohnung
float [fləʊt]	schwimmen, treiben (to float)
floor [flɔːʳ]	die Etage
floor tiles [flɔːʳ] [taɪlz]	die Bodenfliesen (flore tile = die Bodenfliese)
foal [fəʊl]	das Fohlen
food [fuːd]	das Futter, das Essen

for [fɔːʳ]	für, seit
for hours [fɔːʳ] ['auɪz]	stundenlang (hour = die Stunde)
for you [fɔːʳ] [juː]	für dich
forest ['fɒrɪst]	der Wald
fortunately ['fɔːtʃənɪtlɪ]	zum Glück, glücklicherweise
found [faund]	fand (to find = finden), gefunden
four [fɔːʳ]	vier
fourth [fɔːθ]	vierter, vierte
free [friː]	frei
free of [friː] [ɒv]	frei von, erlöst sein
fresh [freʃ]	frisch(e, er, es)
Friday ['fraɪdɪ]	der Freitag
fridge [frɪdʒ]	der Kühlschrank
friend [frend]	die Freundin, der Freund
frightened ['fraɪtnd]	ängstlich
from [frɒm]	von
front door [frɒnt] [dɔːʳ]	die Haustür, die Wohnungstür
full [fʊl]	voll
fun [fʌn]	das Vergnügen, der Spaß

g

gate [geɪt]	das Tor
gave [geɪv]	schenkte, gab (to give = schenken, geben)
gazed at [geɪzd] [æt]	starrte … an (to gaze at = anstarren)
get [get]	bekommen (to get)
(to) get to a place [tuː][get][tuː][eɪ][pleɪs]	einen Ort erreichen

get hold of [get] [həʊld] [ɒv]	herankommen an, erlangen
ghosts [gəʊsts]	Gespenster (ghost = das Gespenst)
girls [gɜːlz]	die Mädchen (girl = das Mädchen)
give [gɪv]	geben (to give)
give up [gɪv] [ʌp]	aufgeben
glade [gleɪd]	die Lichtung
go [gəʊ]	gehen (to go)
go back [gəʊ][bæk]	zurückgehen (to go back)
go riding [gəʊ] ['raɪdɪŋ]	reiten gehen (to go riding)
go round [gəʊ] [raʊnd]	mach eine Runde (durch, um)
go shopping [gəʊ]['ʃɒpɪŋ]	einkaufen gehen (to go shopping)
go to sleep [gəʊ] [tuː] [sliːp]	einschlafen (to go to sleep)
goes dancing [gəʊz] ['dɑːnsɪŋ]	er, sie, es tanzt herum (to go dancing = herumtanzen)
goes on [gəʊz] [ɒn]	geht weiter (to go on = weitergehen)
going ['gəʊɪŋ]	gehen (to go)
going around ['gəʊɪŋ] [ə'raʊnd]	sich herumtreiben, herumgehen (to go around)
going to bed ['gəʊɪŋ] [tuː] [bed]	ins Bett gehen (to go to bed = ins Bett gehen)
going to do ['gəʊɪŋ][tuː][duː]	etwas machen werden (to go)
good [gʊd]	gut
got [gɒt]	bekam (to get = bekommen)

got into [gɒt] ['ɪntʊ] geriet in … hinein (to get into = hineingeraten)

got on Mum's nerves [gɒt] [ɒn] [mʌmz] [nɜːvz] regte Mama auf (to get on sb's nerves = jemanden aufregen)

got rid of [gɒt] [rɪd] [ɒv] wurde los (to get rid of = loswerden)

granny ['grænɪ] die Oma

grass [graːs] das Gras

greaseproof paper ['griːspruːf]['peɪpəʳ] das Butterbrotpapier

great [greɪt] toll, groß(artig)

grins [grɪnz] er, sie, es grinst (to grin = grinsen)

grumbles ['grʌmblz] er, sie, es motzt (to grumble = motzen, murren, schimpfen)

h

had [hæd] hatte(n) (to have = haben)

had made a mess [hæd] [meɪd] [ə] [mes] hatten versaut (to make a mess = etwas versauen)

had peeled off [hæd] [piːld] [ɒf] hatte sich abgelöst (to peel off = sich ablösen)

had to [hæd] [tuː] musste, mussten (to have to = müssen)

hand [hænd] die Hand

hands [hændz] die Hände (hand = die Hand)

happened ['hæpənd] passierte, geschah (to happen = passieren, geschehen)

happily ['hæpɪlɪ] fröhlich, glücklich, vergnügt

happy ['hæpɪ] fröhlich, glücklich

hard [hɑːd]	fest, angestrengt, hart
has [hæz]	er, sie, es hat (to have = haben)
has been [hæz] [biːn]	er, sie, es war, ist gewesen (to be = sein)
has been waiting [hæz][biːn]['weɪtɪŋ]	er, sie, es hat gewartet (to have been waiting = gewartet haben)
hasn't ['hæznt]	er, sie, es hat nicht (Kurzform von: has not)
have [hæv]	haben (to have)
have been (built) [hæv] [biːn] [bɪlt]	sind (aufgebaut)
have fun [hæv][fʌn]	Spaß haben
have to [hæv] [tuː]	müssen (to have to)
have to have a cry [hæv][tuː][hæv][ə][kraɪ]	weinen müssen (to have to)
haven't ['hævnt]	nicht haben (Kurzform von: have not)
he [hiː]	er
he'd made [hiːd] [meɪd]	hatte angestellt (Kurzform von: he had)
he'd soon see [hiːd] [suːn] [siː]	würde er schnell merken
he's [hiːz]	er ist (Kurzform von: he is)
head [hed]	der Kopf
headfirst ['hedfɜːst]	kopfüber
hears [hɪəz]	er, sie, es hört (to hear = hören)
help [help]	helfen (to help)

(is) helping [ɪz] ['helpɪŋ]	er, sie, es hilft, helfen (to help)
her [hɜːˈ]	ihr(e)
here [hɪəˈ]	hier
herself [hɜːˈself]	sich selbst (sie)
high [haɪ]	hoch
him [hɪm]	ihm, ihn
himself [hɪmˈself]	sich selbst (er)
his [hɪz]	sein(e)
hisses ['hɪsɪz]	er, sie, es faucht (to hiss = fauchen)
hits [hɪts]	er, sie, es trifft (to hit = treffen)
hold [həʊld]	halt (to hold = halten)
home [həʊm]	zu Hause
hook [hʊk]	der Haken
hooves [huːvz]	die Hufe (hoof = der Huf)
hopping mad ['hɒpɪŋ] [mæd]	fuchsteufelswild
hops [hɒps]	er, sie, es hoppelt (to hop = hoppeln)
horse [hɔːs]	das Pferd
house [haʊs]	das Haus
how [haʊ]	wie
how it came about [haʊ] [ɪt] [keɪm] [əˈbaʊt]	das kam so
howling ['haʊlɪŋ]	jaulen (to howl)
huge [hjuːdʒ]	riesig
hundred ['hʌndrɪd]	(ein)hundert

I [aɪ]	ich
I am [aɪ] [æm]	ich bin
I'd [aɪd]	ich würde (Kurzform von: I would)
I'll be [aɪl] [biː]	ich werde sein (Kurzform von: I will)
I'm [aɪm]	ich bin (Kurzform von: I am)
I've got [aɪv] [gɒt]	ich habe (Kurzform von: I have)
idea [aɪˈdɪə]	die Idee, der Einfall
idiot [ˈɪdɪət]	der Bescheuerte, der Idiot
if [ɪf]	falls, ob, wenn
imagined [ɪˈmædʒɪnd]	sich vorgestellt (to imagine = sich vorstellen)
immediately [ɪˈmiːdɪətlɪ]	sofort
in [ɪn]	in, im
in despair [ɪn] [dɪˈspɛəˈ]	verzweifelt
in front of [ɪn] [frʌnt] [ɒv]	vor
in order to [ɪn] [ˈɔːdəˈ] [tuː]	um zu
in surprise [ɪn] [səˈpraɪz]	verwundert, überrascht
in the end [ɪn] [ðiː] [end]	schließlich
instead of [ɪnˈsted] [ɒv]	statt
instructor [ɪnˈstrʌktəˈ]	der Lehrer, der Trainer
into [ˈɪntʊ]	in … hinein
is [ɪz]	er, sie, es ist (to be = sein)
is about to [ɪz][əˈbaʊt][tuː]	er, sie, es ist im Begriff (to be about to = im Begriff sein)
isn't [ˈɪznt]	er, sie, es ist nicht (Kurzform von: is not)

it [ɪt]	es
it'll ['ɪtl]	es wird (Kurzform von: it will)
it'll only take a minute ['ɪtl] ['əʊnlɪ] [teik] [ə] ['mɪnɪt]	es dauert nur eine Minute
it's [ɪts]	es ist (Kurzform von: it is)
its [ɪts]	sein, seine, ihr, ihre
jealous ['dʒeləs]	neidisch, eifersüchtig
jeans [dʒiːnz]	die Jeans
jelly babies ['dʒelɪ]['beɪbɪz]	die Gummibärchen (jelly baby = das Gummibärchen)
joyfully ['dʒɔɪfəlɪ]	fröhlich
juice [dʒuːs]	der Saft
jump [dʒʌmp]	springen (to jump)
just [dʒʌst]	genau, ebenso, nur, gerade
keeps [kiːps]	er, sie, es macht weiter (to keep = weitermachen)
keeps stroking [kiːps]['strəʊkɪŋ]	er, sie, es streichelt weiter (to keep stroking = weiterstreicheln)
ketchup bottles ['ketʃəp] [bɒtlz]	die Ketchupflaschen (ketchup bottle = die Ketchupflasche)
kidnapped ['kɪdnæpd]	entführt
kind [kaɪnd]	die Sorte, die Art
kind [kaɪnd]	freundlich, nett
kitchen ['kɪtʃən]	die Küche

kitchen table ['kɪtʃən] ['teɪbl] der Küchentisch

kneeling ['niːlɪŋ] kniet (to kneel = knien)

knew [njuː] wusste (to know = wissen)

knocks over [nɒks]['əʊvəʳ] er, sie, es wirft um (to knock over = umwerfen)

know [nəʊ] kenne (to know = kennen, wissen)

l

label ['leɪbl] das Etikett

label-collecting ['leɪbl] [kə'lektɪŋ] die Etiketten-Sammelei

lady ['leɪdɪ] die Dame

laid [leɪd] legte (to lay = legen)

large [lɑːdʒ] groß

last [lɑːst] letzte(r, s)

later ['leɪtəʳ] später

laughs [lɑːfs] er, sie, es lacht (to laugh = lachen)

lead [liːd] führen (to lead)

leaps [liːps] er, sie, es springt (to leap = springen)

leash [liːʃ] die Leine

leaving ['liːvɪŋ] hinterlassen, zurück-lassen (to leave = hinter-lassen, zurücklassen)

legs [legz] die Beine (leg = das Bein)

lemonade bottles ['leməneɪd] ['bɒtlz] die Limonadenflaschen (lemonade bottle = die Limonadenflasche)

let [let] ließ (to let = lassen)

let starve [let][staːv]	verhungern lassen (to let starve)
licence disc ['laɪsəns][dɪsk]	die Hundemarke
licking ['lɪkɪŋ]	lecken (to lick)
licks [lɪks]	er, sie, es leckt (to lick = lecken)
lie [laɪ]	liegen (to lie)
light [laɪt]	der Schein, das Licht
like [laɪk]	wie (like that = wie das)
like [laɪk]	mögen (to like)
like to [laɪk] [tuː]	gern wollen (to like to)
liqueur bottles [lɪ'kjʊəʳ] ['bɒtlz]	die Likörflaschen (liqueur bottle = die Likörflasche)
little ['lɪtl]	klein(e, er, es)
little one ['lɪtl] [wʌn]	der, die, das Kleine
locks [lɒks]	er, sie, es schließt (to lock = schließen)
lonely ['ləʊnlɪ]	alleine
long [lɒŋ]	lang(e, er, es)
longer ['lɒŋəʳ]	länger
look [lʊk]	aussehen, schauen (to look)
looks [lʊks]	er, sie, es sieht aus (to look = aussehen)
looks at [lʊks][æt]	er, sie, es sieht an (to look at = ansehen)
lose [luːs]	verlieren (to lose)
loves [lʌvz]	er, sie, es liebt (to love = lieben)
lovingly ['lʌvɪŋlɪ]	liebevoll

luckily ['lʌkɪlɪ]　　　　　　　zum Glück

lucky ['lʌkɪ]　　　　　　　　Glück haben (to be lucky)

m

made out of　　　　　　　　aufgebaut aus, hergestellt
[meɪd] [aʊt] [ɒv]　　　　　aus … (to make out of =
　　　　　　　　　　　　　herstellen)

makes [meɪks]　　　　　　　er, sie, es macht
　　　　　　　　　　　　　(to make = machen)

man [mæn]　　　　　　　　der Mann, der Mensch

manage ['mænɪdʒ]　　　　　schaffen (to manage)

mare [mɛəʳ]　　　　　　　　die Stute

margarine ['mɑːdʒəˈriːn]　die Margarine

master ['mɑːstəʳ]　　　　　der Herr
　　　　　　　　　　　　　(hier: das Herrchen)

may [meɪ]　　　　　　　　　können

maybe ['meɪbiː]　　　　　　vielleicht

me [miː]　　　　　　　　　　mich, mir

means [miːnz]　　　　　　　er, sie, es bedeutet
　　　　　　　　　　　　　(to mean = bedeuten)

men [men]　　　　　　　　　die Männer
　　　　　　　　　　　　　(man = der Mann)

mess [mes]　　　　　　　　der Unfug, das Durcheinander

middle ['mɪdl]　　　　　　　die Mitte, mitten

might [maɪt]　　　　　　　　könnten

minute ['mɪnɪt]　　　　　　die Minute

mistress ['mɪstrɪs]　　　　die Herrin
　　　　　　　　　　　　　(hier: das Frauchen)

moment ['məʊmənt]　　　　der Moment

Monday ['mʌndɪ]　　　　　der Montag

money ['mʌnɪ]　　　　　　　das Geld

more [mɔːʳ]　　　　　　　　mehr

morning ['mɔːnɪŋ]	der Morgen
mother ['mʌðəʳ]	die Mutter
much [mʌtʃ]	viel
mum [mʊm]	die Mama
mummy ['mʌmɪ]	die Mama
murmered ['mɜːməd]	murmelte, murrte (to murmur = murmeln, murren)
must [mʌst]	muss, musst, müssen, müsst
mustn't ['mʌsnt]	nicht dürfen (Kurzform von: must not)
muzzle ['mʌzl]	das Maul
my [maɪ]	mein, meine
name [neɪm]	der Name
naughty ['nɔːtɪ]	ungezogen
nearly ['nɪəlɪ]	fast
neck [nek]	der Hals
need [niːd]	brauchen (to need)
need to … [niːd] [tuː]	müssen (to need to …)
neighbour ['neɪbəʳ]	der Nachbar
nervously ['nɜːvəslɪ]	aufgeregt, ängstlich
never [nevəʳ]	nie
new [njuː]	neu(e, er, es)
next to [nekst][tuː]	neben
nice [naɪs]	hübsch, nett, lieb
nicer [naɪsəʳ]	netter (nice = nett)
night [naɪt]	die Nacht
no [nəʊ]	nein, nicht, kein(e)

no longer [nəʊ]['lɒŋəʳ]	nicht mehr
nobody ['nəʊbədɪ]	niemand
nod [nɒd]	nicken (to nod)
nods [nɒdz]	er, sie, es nickt (to nod = nicken)
noises ['nɔɪzɪz]	die Geräusche (noise = das Geräusch)
normally ['nɔːməlɪ]	üblich(erweise), normal(erweise)
not [nɒt]	nicht
not as good as [nɒt] [æz] [gud] [æz]	nicht so gut wie
nothing ['nʌθɪŋ]	nichts
nothing but ['nʌθɪŋ] [bʌt]	nichts außer
notice! ['nəʊtɪs]	Bekanntmachung!
now [naʊ]	jetzt, nun

o

obstacles ['ɒbsteklz]	die Hindernisse (obstacle = das Hindernis)
obvious ['ɒbvɪəs]	offensichtlich
of [ɒv]	von
of course [ɒv][kɔːs]	natürlich
off [ɒf]	von, weg
oh dear! [əʊ] [dɪəʳ]	oje!
oil bottles [ɔɪl] ['bɒtlz]	die Ölflaschen (oil bottle = die Ölflasche)
OK ['əʊ'keɪ]	O. K., in Ordnung
old [əʊld]	alt
older ['əʊldəʳ]	älter (old = alt)
on [ɒn]	auf, an

on his own [ɒn][hɪz][əʊn]	ganz allein
on the phone [ɒn] [ðə] [fəʊn]	am Telefon
one [wʌn]	ein(e, r, s)
one another [wʌn] [ə'nʌðəʳ]	einander
one label of each kind [wʌn] ['leɪbl] [ɒv] [itʃ] [kaɪnd]	von jedem Etikett nur eines
only ['əʊnlɪ]	nur
onto ['ɒntʊ]	auf
open ['əʊpən]	öffnen (to open)
opening ['əʊpənɪŋ]	(er)öffnet (to open = (er)öffnen)
or [ɔːʳ]	oder
orphan ['ɔːfən]	die Waise
orphan dog ['ɔːfən][dɒg]	der Waisenhund
other ['ʌðəʳ]	anderer, andere, anderes
our ['aʊəʳ]	unser, unsere, unseres
out [aʊt]	aus, heraus, hinaus
out of [aʊt] [ɒv]	aus … heraus, hinaus
out of love [aʊt] [ɒv] [lʌv]	aus Liebe
outside ['aʊt'saɪd]	draußen
outside the door ['aʊt'saɪd] [ðə] [dɔːʳ]	vor die Tür, vor der Tür
oven ['ʌvn]	der Herd
over ['əʊvəʳ]	über
over them ['əʊvəʳ] [ðem]	darüber, über sie hinweg
over there ['əʊvəʳ] [ðɛəʳ]	da drüben
overflowing ['əʊvəfləʊiŋ]	randvoll

pack [pæk]	(ein)packen (to pack)
paper [ˈpeɪpəʳ]	das Papier
passage [ˈpæsɪdʒ]	der Gang
path [pɑːθ]	der Weg
paying attention to [ˈpeɪɪŋ] [əˈtenʃən] [tuː]	sich kümmern um (to pay attention to)
peace [piːs]	der Frieden
peeled off [piːld] [ɒf]	löste sich ab (to peel off = sich ablösen)
people [ˈpiːpl]	die Leute, die Menschen
perfect [ˈpɜːfɪkt]	perfekt, in bester Ordnung
perhaps [pəˈhæps]	vielleicht
person [ˈpɜːsn]	der Mensch, die Person
phone [fəʊn]	das Telefon (Kurzform von: telephone)
pictures [ˈpɪktʃəʳz]	die Bilder (picture = das Bild)
piece [piːs]	das Stück
pile [paɪl]	der Stapel, Haufen
play [pleɪ]	spielen (to play)
plays [pleɪz]	er, sie, es spielt (to play = spielen)
police [pəˈliːs]	die Polizei
ponies [ˈpəʊnɪz]	die Ponys (pony = das Pony)
pony [ˈpəʊnɪ]	das Pony
pony farm [ˈpəʊnɪ] [fɑːm]	der Ponyhof
poor [pʊəʳ]	arm
praised [preɪzd]	lobte (to praise = loben)

prefers [prɪˈfɜːˈz] — er, sie, es mag lieber (to prefer = lieber mögen)

pregnant [ˈpregnənt] — trächtig, schwanger

present [ˈpresənt] — das Geschenk

pretty [ˈprɪtɪ] — hübsch

prickly [ˈprɪklɪ] — piksig

proud of [praʊd] [ɒf] — stolz auf

proudly [ˈpraʊdlɪ] — stolz

pull [pʊl] — ziehen (to pull)

pull loose [pʊl][luːs] — losreißen (to pull loose)

pullover [pʊlˈəʊvəˈ] — der Pullover

pulls [pʊlz] — er, sie, es zieht (to pull = ziehen)

pulls ... off [pʊlz] [ɒv] — er, sie, es zieht ... weg (to pull off = wegziehen)

pulls a face [pʊlz][eɪ][feɪs] — er, sie, es macht ein Gesicht (to pull a face = ein Gesicht machen)

pulls himself free [pʊlz][hɪmˈself][friː] — er, sie, es reißt sich los (to pull oneself free = sich losreißen)

pushes [ˈpʊʃɪz] — er, sie, es schiebt (to push = schieben)

put [pʊt] — stellen, setzen, legen (to put)

puts [pʊts] — er, sie, es legt (to put = setzen, stellen, legen)

puts on [pʊts] [ɒn] — er, sie, es macht an (to put on = anmachen)

q

quiet [ˈkwaɪət] — die Ruhe, ruhig

quite [kwaɪt] — ganz, ziemlich

rabbit ['ræbɪt]	das Kaninchen
ran some water into [ræn] [sʌm] ['wɔːtə'] ['ɪntʊ]	ließ etwas Wasser in … hineinlaufen (to run something into = etwas in etwas hineinlaufen lassen)
read [red]	las (to read [riːd] = lesen)
real [rɪəl]	echt(e, er, es)
really ['rɪəlɪ]	echt, wirklich
really miserable ['rɪəlɪ] ['mɪzərəbl]	kreuzunglücklich
red [red]	rot(e, r, s)
relieved [rɪ'liːvd]	erleichtert
resolutely ['rezəluːtlɪ]	entschlossen
rest [rest]	der Rest
result [rɪ'zʌlt]	das Resultat, das Ergebnis
ride [raɪd]	reiten (to ride)
rides [raɪdz]	er, sie, es reitet (to ride = reiten)
riding ['raɪdɪŋ]	reiten (to ride)
riding helmets ['raɪdɪŋ] ['helmɪts]	Reitkappen (riding helmet = die Reitkappe)
right [raɪt]	so, also, richtig
robber ['rɒbə']	der Dieb
round [raʊnd]	in … herum, um
rub down [rʌb] [daʊn]	abreiben, striegeln (to rub down)
rubbish ['rʌbɪʃ]	Abfall, unnützes Zeug
rubbish bin ['rʌbɪʃ] [bɪn]	der Abfalleimer
rubbish tip ['rʌbɪʃ] [tɪp]	der Müllplatz

runs [rʌnz]	er, sie, es läuft (to run = laufen)
rushes ['rʌʃɪz]	er, sie, es flitzt (to rush = flitzen)
sacrifice ['sækrɪfaɪs]	das Opfer
sad [sæd]	traurig
saddle ['sædl]	der Sattel
saddle up ['sædl] [ʌp]	satteln (to saddle up)
saddles ['sædlz]	die Sättel (saddle = der Sattel)
said [sed]	sagte (to say = sagen)
same [seɪm]	gleich
saved [seɪvd]	gerettet, erlöst (to save = retten, erlösen)
saw [sɔː]	sah (to see = sehen)
say [seɪ]	sagen (to say)
says [sez]	er, sie, es sagt (to say = sagen)
schnapps [ʃnæps]	der Schnaps
scrape [skreɪp]	auskratzen (to scrape)
see [siː]	sehen (to see)
see for yourself [siː][fɔːʳ][jɔːˮself]	selbst sehen (to see)
sees [siːz]	er, sie, es sieht (to see = sehen)
seriously ['sɪərɪəslɪ]	ernst
sets [sets]	(die Sonne) geht unter (to set = untergehen)
setting up ['setɪŋ] [ʌp]	eröffnen (to set up)
seven ['sevn]	sieben

shakes [ʃeɪks]	er, sie, es schüttelt (to shake = schütteln)
shall [ʃæl]	sollen
she [ʃiː]	sie
she's [ʃiːz]	sie ist (Kurzform von: she is)
She's all right. [ʃiːz] [ɔːl] [raɪt]	Ihr ist nichts passiert.
sheet of paper [ʃiːt] [ɒv] [ˈpeɪpəʳ]	das Blatt Papier
shines [ʃaɪnz]	er, sie, es scheint (to shine = scheinen)
shining [ˈʃaɪnɪŋ]	leuchten, strahlen, scheinen (to shine)
shop [ʃɒp]	das Geschäft
shopping [ˈʃɒpɪŋ]	einkaufen (to shop)
should [ʃʊd]	soll(en), sollte(n)
sick [sɪk]	krank, speiübel
side [saɪd]	die Seite
sighed [saɪd]	seufzte (to sigh = seufzen)
silently [ˈsaɪləntlɪ]	geräuschlos
silliest [ˈsɪlɪəst]	dümmste(r, s) (silly = dumm, albern, doof)
simply [ˈsɪmplɪ]	einfach
sink [sɪnk]	das Spülbecken
sisters [ˈsɪstəʳz]	die Schwestern (sister = die Schwester)
sits [sɪts]	er, sie, es sitzt (to sit = sitzen)
sleep [sliːp]	schlafen (to sleep)
slightly [ˈslaɪtlɪ]	leicht

slipped off [slɪpt] [ɒf]	lösten sich ab (von) (to slip off = sich ablösen (von))
slowly ['sləʊlɪ]	langsam
small [smɔːl]	klein
smell [smel]	der Geruch, der Duft
sneers [snɪəz]	er, sie, es höhnt (to sneer = höhnen)
so [səʊ]	so, deshalb, also
soaking wet ['səʊkiŋ] [wet]	klatschnass
soft [sɒft]	weich
some [sʌm]	etwas, einige, manche
someone ['sʌmwʌn]	(irgend)jemand
something ['sʌmθɪŋ]	(irgend)etwas
sometimes ['sʌmtaɪmz]	manchmal
son [sʌn]	der Sohn
soon [suːn]	(schon) bald
sort [sɔːt]	die Art, die Sorte
sort of beer [sɔːt] [ɒv] [bɪəʳ]	die Biersorte
spare time [spɛəʳ] [taɪm]	die Freizeit
spent [spent]	verbrachte (to spend = verbringen)
spot [spɒt]	der Platz, die Stelle
spreads [spreds]	er, sie, es streut (to spread = streuen)
stable ['steɪbl]	der Stall
stalls [stɔːlz]	die Boxen (stall = die Box)
stamps [stæmps]	die Briefmarken (stamp = die Briefmarke)
stand up [stænd] [ʌp]	aufstehen (to stand up)

standing ['stændɪŋ] — standen (to stand = stehen)

start [staːt] — beginnen, anfangen (to start)

started ['staːtɪd] — begann, fing an (to start = beginnen, anfangen)

startled ['staːrtld] — erschrocken

starts [staːts] — er, sie, es fängt an (to start = anfangen)

starve [staːv] — verhungern (to starve)

stay [steɪ] — bleiben (to stay)

stays [steɪz] — er, sie, es bleibt (to stay = bleiben)

steal [stiːl] — klauen, stehlen (to steal)

sticking ['stɪkɪŋ] — rausstrecken (to stick)

still [stɪl] — noch

stole [stəʊl] — stahl (to steal = stehlen)

stolen ['stəʊlən] — gestohlen

stop [stɒp] — aufhören (to stop)

stops [stɒps] — er, sie, es hält an (to stop = anhalten)

stories ['stɔːrɪz] — Geschichten (story = die Geschichte)

straight away [streɪt] [əˈweɪ] — gleich, sofort, geradewegs

strange [streɪndʒ] — seltsam(e, er, es)

stranger ['streɪndʒəʳ] — der Fremde

straw [strɔː] — das Stroh

stream [striːm] — der Bach

stress [stres] — der Stress

stroking ['strəʊkɪŋ] — streicheln (to stroke)

stuck [stʌk]	klebte, steckte (to stick = kleben, stecken)
stupid ['stjuːpɪd]	blöde, dumm
such [sʌtʃ]	solch(e, n), so ein(e, s)
suddenly ['sʌdnlɪ]	plötzlich
sun [sʌn]	die Sonne
Sunday ['sʌndɪ]	der Sonntag
super ['suːpəʳ]	super
super collection ['suːpəʳ] [kəˈlekʃən]	eine super Sammlung
supermarket ['suːpəɱaːkɪt]	der Supermarkt
supper ['sʌpəʳ]	das Abendessen
suppose [səˈpəʊz]	annehmen (to suppose)
sure [ʃʊəʳ]	sicher
surely ['ʃʊəlɪ]	bestimmt
sweetly ['swiːtlɪ]	süß

t

tail [teɪl]	der Schwanz
take [teɪk]	nimm, trag (to take = nehmen, tragen)
take a bath [teɪk] [ə] [baːθ]	baden (to take)
take for a walk [teɪk][fɔːʳ][ə][wɔːk]	spazieren gehen mit (to take)
take off [teɪk] [ɒv]	ab-, weg-, herunter- nehmen (to take off)
take someone's side [teɪk]['sʌmwʌnz][saɪd]	Partei ergreifen für (to take)

takes after [teɪks] ['ɑːftəʳ]	er, sie, es ähnelt, ist aus dem gleichen Holz geschnitzt wie (to take after = ähneln)
taking [teɪkɪŋ]	nehmen (to take = nehmen)
talk [tɔːk]	sprechen (to talk)
talk rubbish [tɔːk]['rʌbɪʃ]	dummes Zeug reden (to talk rubbish)
talking ['tɔːkɪŋ]	(be)sprechen, reden (to talk)
taught [tɔːt]	beigebracht (to teach = beibringen)
teeth [tiːθ]	die Zähne (tooth = der Zahn)
telephone ['telɪfəʊn]	das Telefon
tell [tel]	erzählen (to tell)
tell me! [tel] [miː]	sag schon!
tells [telz]	er, sie, es sagt (to tell = sagen)
terrible trouble ['terəbəl] ['trʌbl]	der Riesenärger
than [ðæn]	als
that [ðæt]	das(s), die
that's [ðæts]	das ist (Kurzform von: that is)
That's all right with me. [ðæts] [ɔːl] [raɪt] [wɪð] [miː]	Meinetwegen.
the [ðə]	der, die, das
the two of them [ðə] [tuː] [ɒv] [ðəm]	die beiden
their [ðɛəʳ]	ihr(e, n)

them [ðem]	ihnen, sie
themselves [ðəm'selvz]	sich (Mehrzahl)
then [ðen]	dann
there [ðɛɚ']	da, dort
there are [ðɛə'][ɑː']	da sind, es gibt (to be)
there's [ðɛə'z]	dort ist, es gibt (Kurzform von: there is)
they [ðeɪ]	sie (Mehrzahl)
they'll [ðeɪl]	sie werden (Kurzform von: they will)
they're [ðeɪ']	sie sind (Kurzform von: they are)
thief [θiːf]	der Dieb
thing [θɪŋ]	die Sache
think [θɪnk]	denke (to think = denken)
thinking ['θɪŋkɪŋ]	denken (to think)
thinks [θɪŋkz]	er, sie, es denkt (to think = denken)
thirsty ['θɜːstɪ]	durstig
this [ðɪs]	dies(e, r, s)
this one's [ðɪs] [wʌnz]	diese (r, s) ist (Kurzform von: this one is)
this one's got [ðɪs][wʌnz][gɒt]	diese (r, s) hier hat (Kurzform von: this one has got)
those [ðəʊz]	diese, jene, solche
though [ðəʊ]	obwohl
thought [θɔːt]	dachte, überlegte (to think = denken, überlegen)

thought about [θɔːt] [əˈbaʊt]	überlegte, dachte nach (to think about = überlegen, nachdenken)
thoughtful [ˈθɔːtfʊl]	nachdenklich
thoughts [θɔːts]	die Gedanken (thought = der Gedanke)
three [θriː]	drei
through [θruː]	durch (… hindurch)
throws [θrəʊz]	er, sie, es wirft (to throw = werfen)
tie [taɪ]	anbinden, festbinden (to tie)
tied up [taɪd][ʌp]	angebunden (to tie up = anbinden)
tight [taɪt]	fest
time [taɪm]	die Zeit
times [taɪmz]	die Male (time = das Mal)
tiptoe [ˈtɪptəʊ]	auf Zehenspitzen gehen (to tiptoe)
tired [ˈtaɪəd]	müde
to [tuː]	nach, zu
to be [tuː] [biː]	zu sein
to dry [tuː] [draɪ]	zum Trocknen (to dry = trocknen)
together [təˈgeðəˈ]	zusammen
tomorrow [təˈmɒrəʊ]	morgen
tongue [tʌŋ]	die Zunge
too [tuː]	auch, zu (sehr)
took [tʊk]	holte, nahm (to take = holen, nehmen)

took Rudi's side [tʊk] ['ruːdiz] [saɪd]	nahm Rudi in Schutz (to take someone's side = jemanden in Schutz nehmen)
torch [tɔːtʃ]	die Taschenlampe
total ['təʊtl]	total(e, r, s)
touch [tʌtʃ]	anfassen, berühren (to touch)
track [træk]	der Weg
trainer ['treɪnəʳ]	der Turnschuh
translated [trænz'leɪtɪd]	übersetzt (to translate = übersetzen)
tree [triː]	der Baum
trivialities [ɥtrɪvɪ'ælɪtɪz]	der Kleinkram
trot [trɒt]	traben (to trot)
trouble ['trʌbl]	der Ärger, die Schwierigkeiten
trunks [trʌnks]	die Stämme (trunk = der Stamm)
tub [tʌb]	die Wanne
Tuesday ['tjuːzdɪ]	der Dienstag
two [tuː]	zwei

u

uncle ['ʌnkl]	der Onkel
unfortunately [ʌn'fɔːtʃnɪtlɪ]	leider
unhooks [ʌn'hʊks]	er, sie, es bindet los (to unhook = losbinden)
untie [ʌn'taɪ]	losbinden (to untie)
until [ʌn'tɪl]	bis
up [ʌp]	oben
upset [ʌp'set]	traurig

us [ʌs]	uns
usual ['juːʒuəl]	gewöhnlich, normal

V

very ['verɪ]	sehr
vet [vet]	der Tierarzt (Kurzform von: veterinarian)
vinegar bottles ['vɪnegəʳ] ['bɒtlz]	die Essigflaschen (vinegar bottle = die Essigflasche)
visitors ['vɪzɪtəz]	die Besucher (visitor = der Besucher)

W

wag [wæg]	wedeln (to wag)
wagging ['wægɪŋ]	wedeln (to wag)
wags [wægz]	er, sie, es wedelt (to wag = wedeln)
wait [weɪt]	warten (to wait)
waiting ['weɪtɪŋ]	warten (to wait)
waiting in order to ['weɪtɪŋ][ɪn]['ɔːdəʳ] [tuː]	darauf warten, etwas zu tun (to wait)
wake ... up [weɪk] ... [ʌp]	wecken, aufwachen (to wake up)
wake up! [weɪk] [ʌp]	wach auf! (to wake up = aufwachen)
walk [wɔːk]	gehen (to walk), der Spaziergang
want [wɒnt]	will (to want = wollen)
want [wɒnt]	wollen (to want)
wanted ['wɒntɪd]	wollte (to want = wollen)
wants [wɒnts]	er, sie, es will (to want = wollen)

warm [wɒːm]	warm
was [wɒz]	er, sie, es war, wurde (to be = sein)
washed clean [wɔːʃt] [kliːn]	wusch sauber (to wash clean = sauber waschen)
wasn't ['wɒznt]	war nicht (Kurzform von: was not)
watch [wɒtʃ]	gucken, sehen (to watch)
watching ['wɒtʃɪŋ]	gucken, sehen (to watch)
watching TV ['wɒtʃɪŋ] ['tiːviː]	fernzusehen (to watch TV = fernsehen)
water ['wɔːtəʳ]	das Wasser
waves [weɪvz]	er, sie, es winkt (to wave = winken)
way [weɪ]	der Weg
we [wiː]	wir
we'll [wiːl]	wir werden (Kurzform von: we will)
we've [wiːv]	wir haben (Kurzform von: we have)
Wednesday ['wenzdɪ]	der Mittwoch
well [wel]	gut
went [went]	ging (to go = gehen)
went a little red [went] [ə] ['lɪtl] [red]	wurde ein bisschen rot (to go red = rot werden)
went on collecting [went] [ɒn] [kə'lektɪŋ]	sammelte weiter (to go on collecting = weitersammeln)
were [wɜː]	waren, wären (to be = sein)
were any good [wɜː] ['enɪ] [gʊd]	taugte etwas (to be any good = etwas taugen)

wet [wet]	nass
what [wɒt]	was, welche(r, s)
what a load of rubbish! [wɒt] [ə] [ləʊd] [ɒv] [ˈrʌbɪʃ]	so ein Mist!
what about …? [wɒt] [əˈbaʊt]	wie wär's mit …?
What are you doing here? [wɒt] [ɑːˈ] [juː] [ˈduːɪŋ] [hɪəˈ]	Was macht ihr hier?
What does … mean? [wɒt] [dʌz] [miːn]	Was bedeutet …?
what's [wɒts]	was ist (Kurzform von: what is)
what's the matter? [wɒts] [ðə] [ˈmætəˈ]	was ist los?
whatever [wɒtˈevəˈ]	was (immer)
when [wen]	wenn, als
whenever [wenˈevəˈ]	(wann) immer
where [wɛəˈ]	wo
where it belongs [ˈwɛəˈ] [ɪt] [bɪˈlɒŋz]	wo es hingehört
whether [ˈweðəˈ]	ob
which [wɪtʃ]	welcher, welche, welches
while [waɪl]	die Weile
whispers [ˈwɪspəz]	er, sie, es flüstert (to whisper = flüstern)
white [waɪt]	weiß(e, er, es)
who [huː]	wer
whole [həʊl]	ganz(e, r, s)
wildly [ˈwaɪldlɪ]	wild
will [wɪl]	werde(n, t), wirst, wird

will be [wɪl] [biː]	wird … sein (to be = sein)
will be saved [wɪl] [biː] [seɪvd]	bleibt … erspart (to be saved = erspart bleiben)
will help you [wɪl] [help] [juː]	wird euch helfen (to help = helfen)
window ['wɪndəʊ]	das Fenster
wine bottles [waɪn] ['bɒtlz]	die Weinflaschen (wine bottle = die Weinflasche)
with [wɪð] [wɪθ]	mit
without [wɪð'aʊt]	ohne
wobbly ['wɒblɪ]	wackelig(e, er, es)
won't [wəʊnt]	will nicht (Kurzform von: will not)
wonderful ['wʌndəfʊl]	wunderschön, herrlich
work [wɜːk]	die Arbeit, das Werk
world [wɜːld]	die Welt
worn out [wɔːn] [aʊt]	fix und fertig, erschöpft
worry ['wʌrɪ]	stören, Sorgen machen
would [wʊd]	würde
would get [wʊd] [get]	bekäme (to get = bekommen)
would have advised [wʊd] [hæv] [əd'vaɪzd]	hätte geraten (to advise = (be)raten)
would like to be [wʊd][laɪk][tuː][biː]	wäre gern (to like to be = gerne sein)
wouldn't ['wʊdnt]	würde nicht (Kurzform von: would not)
wrote [rəʊt]	schrieb (to write = schreiben)

yard [jɑːd]	der Hof
year [jɪəʳ]	das Jahr
yelled [jeld]	schrie (to yell = schreien)
yes [jes]	ja
yesterday [ˈjestədeɪ]	gestern
yet [jet]	noch, bis jetzt
you [juː]	du, dir, dich, ihr, Sie
you're [juːʳ]	du bist (Kurzform von: you are)
you've [juːv]	du hast (Kurzform von: you have)
you've got [juːv] [gɒt]	du hast (Kurzform von: you have got)
your [juːʳ]	dein(e), euer, eure, Ihr
your'e [juːʳ]	du bist (Kurzform von: you are)
yourself [jɔːʳself]	dir, dich, euch